WANDERER

A Collection of Poetry & Prose

Court Young

Cover Design: Islam Farid @islamsfarid
Illustrations: Casey Leef @caseyleefdesign

ISBN: 978-1-7372044-0-4

For Casey, my soul sister and biggest supporter since day one.

Thank you.

Wanderings

Author's Note

2019 was one of the most challenging and turbulent years of my life.

WANDERER tells my story of that year as I traveled to different places – both physically and metaphorically. At the start of the year, I left behind a two-year relationship after reconnecting with a college flame. I spent the summer falling for that flame, had my heart broken, and then ended the year with the best love of them all.

My two-year relationship was one of the darkest periods of my life. I was incredibly unhappy and depressed. I speak often about how I felt numb during those two years and do not remember much – like there is a black hole in my memories of that time. I did not truly realize what life had to offer until I saw an old college ex again, *the Eagle*. I start WANDERER with that moment, because that was the moment when everything changed, when I began to live again.

My story then goes back to the "prequel," if you will, my college days with *the Wolf* and *the Eagle*, before coming back to reconnecting with *the Eagle* again, years later. I tell the tale of how he and I spent a week falling in love in the Pacific Northwest, and how we had no idea what we were doing the rest of that summer as we tried not to fall for each other. Finally, there is a "coming to" moment where I realize that I am better off without him, and that I am greater than my past, which allowed me to truly be able to move on. Moving on was hard, but worth it, for I found love again, with myself but also with a great man.

Each section of WANDERER corresponds to a location, as I wandered through life and love and lust during that year. Places hold memories for me; it is how I see the world. WANDERER will take you on a journey through southwest Virginia; Seattle, Washington; the neighborhoods of Arlington, Virginia; then finally back home to my roots in North Carolina.

I hope you enjoy my story of falling hard and learning to get back up again, and how the greatest love is *yours*. It will come to you.

With love,
Court

Beginning Again in Crystal City

I swear
he was going to kiss me
and what
scared me the most
was that
I wanted him to.

It was over
in an instant
but when our eyes
met again
I saw my future –
our future –
flash before me.
And I wanted it.
More than anything.

COFFEE BREAK

That romantic, cozy smell of roasted coffee hit me when I walked through the door. But all I saw was you: *tall, arrogant, commanding,* in the center of the room. Then you saw me, and later you told me all you felt was happy.

I was shaking and flustered as I ordered, but I don't think you could tell. I knew I was in trouble, *oh, how I knew.* Such a simple thing, really. Two old friends, who used to be more than friends, meeting up for something so normal, so innocent. Little did we know, that was the beginning of everything.

Where can I find you for a cup of coffee?

As winter's frost was ending
and the flowers were starting
on their journey to bloom
I saw you again
in the middle of the city
and realized my heart
had been waiting for you.

Love in a College Town, Southwest Virginia

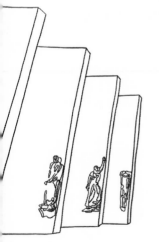

WHEN WE FIRST MET: THE WOLF

How my friend had invited you over and when you walked through our door, my heart skipped a beat. How you came right over to me and introduced yourself—eyes glinting. How when we locked eyes, I could feel the electricity, that magnetic chemistry that I had no idea would get me into trouble later. How you thought to yourself, *damn, she's beautiful.*

You told me
you're beautiful
in the simplest way
and I happened to believe you
until you walked away
and now we are silent
what we had was gone
I thought I would hurt you
in the end I was wrong.

Fuck you for breaking my heart
for whispering lies to my innocent soul
for leading me on like you did.

Fuck you for never responding
and ignoring me like a little child
instead of just saying what you felt.

Fuck you for making me fall
harder than I should
for a boy I thought I knew.

Fuck you.

Love in a College Town, Southwest Virginia

I am scared
of falling again

of not being
good enough

of finding
my heart and soul

and having them
ripped to pieces
shredded to bits

and me crying
so many tears
they could fill
the ocean.

WHEN WE FIRST MET: THE EAGLE

How our two groups of friends merged at that
crowded bar, and yet you still singled me out. How
you led me to the dance floor, despite other girls
vying for your attention. How we were aware of
nothing but our bodies and the music. How you
wanted me to come home with you that night, but I
wanted to make you wait. How back then, I truly
lived for the chase. The funny thing is, we were
always chasing each other *until the very end*.

Falling hard
tumbling
yet holding myself back
on the brink
because I can be
wary of love.

Love in a College Town, Southwest Virginia

You're slowly breaking
down my walls
seeing parts of me
no one has ever seen before.

It terrifies me—
this vulnerability
is not something
I'm used to.

Lying here
I remember how
we used to fuck
on this floor.

And how my body
was beautiful to you.

And how I felt
strong
feminine
unbreakable.

I am thankful

for you
and that the Universe
answered my prayers
when I asked her
to heal my wounds.

I wasn't expecting you
and I wasn't looking for love
but I guess things happen
when you least
expect them to.

Nights in Seattle

The way he
kissed me again
with the hunger of
long lost friends
reunited once more
sparked a fire in me
I forgot I had.

My heart of flame
could turn
even your lead core
into gold.

My love is alchemy.

Nights in Seattle

Your fingers traced
the small of my back
as you brushed your mouth
down the curve of my neck.

"Undress me," I whispered
beneath the red glow
of lust, passion, desire –
while you loved me so.

In a meadow
of purple lupines
overlooking the sea
I glanced at you
when your eyes found me

watching with wonder
maybe love
even though
you would tell me later
I wasn't enough

but in that moment

I was *pure magic.*

I have a heart of fire
and you're afraid
of getting burned.

But you're still
attracted to
my warmth

and you need me
like I need you.

– you're my oxygen

I love
wildly and recklessly at first
often falling
hard and fast.

It's only when
my fire has cooled
do I take a step back
and realize
I shouldn't have done that.

Maybe it's the wild child
inside me?

I wish
you would

love me
the way you do

when you're
drunk.

We broke up
the first time
for a reason
maybe
we were never
meant to be.

Nights in Seattle

"Let's just have fun,"
you said.

How can I
just have fun
when I opened
my heart to you
and you didn't want it?

How can I
just have fun
when I tend to fall
in lust so fast
I mistake it for love?

My spectacular heart
deserves
the greatest love
and *this*
is not it.

What we could have been –

a duet evoking the greatest envy
a radiant pair as we walked our paths together
a summer song forever on repeat –

was not destined in the stars.

Nights in Seattle

Remember me
as a wanderer wild
with brilliant, untamed eyes
and a heart of golden fire.

Lost on the East Coast

You didn't know
how to let
the wild rise in me.

You thought
it was your job
to try and tame me.

You're using me
for your own
emotional needs
because you're afraid
of being alone.

I have my own needs too
and I deserve
so. much. more.
than a man who only loves
when he's lonely.

I feel like my heart
has been ripped out
of my chest by you
and flung to the floor.

But you dropped it
by accident
you didn't know
you. didn't. know.
that you were the one
holding my heart
in your hands.

I cried myself
to sleep last night
tears streaming silently
down my face.
My brain said
he isn't worth it
but my heart wouldn't listen.

I'm still
reeling from you
and it's not fair
that you took
my confidence from me.

I shouldn't be giving you
this much power—
some days I still believe
that you've ruined me.

I'm slowly learning
to let things be
and to stop fighting
for what's not meant
for me.

Thoughts of you
race through my head
I can't make them stop
make. them. stop.

I never want
for anything
to be left unsaid

but the end of us
has muted me.

HEARTBREAK

Heartbreak is the worst kind of roller coaster. There are moments I am fine; then suddenly, I find myself crying uncontrollably. As someone who feels things deeply, when I fall in love, I fall hard and fast. I love with everything I have. So, when my heart breaks, it feels like my heart is shattering into a million pieces. When I try to glue the pieces back together, there is a piece missing. I am no longer whole.

It is not like a room in my heart has closed, but more like a piece of my heart has shattered and fallen off, into the abyss. When your heart breaks, you have to work on filling in that missing piece and forming a scar. You must work on becoming whole again.

There are days
when I feel
secure and sure
of this path
I walk alone.

But some days
my heart
takes over my brain
my emotions
overwhelm me

and I can't help
but think
why can't we
walk this path
together?

I was lost in a field of sunflowers
while you were caught in the rain
our paths crossed momentarily
before the clouds took you away.

I still
write stories
about you
in my head
because
I don't want
to accept
the reality
of us.

I wish I could let
the southern breeze
carry my worries away.

But it only tangles my hair
and leaves knots in my heart
as I silently wish

you were here with me.

Nostalgia
breaks my heart
more than you
ever did.

Memories hurt
much more
than you
leaving.

Missing you
comes in waves.

Sometimes I'm fine
sometimes it hits me so hard
that the floodgates open
and the currents take
my breath away.

The ocean of memories
is drowning me
and I don't know how
to swim in this sea.

My body still craves
your touch
just like my heart
still craves
the words you couldn't say.

If he truly loved you
he wouldn't have
let you walk away.
At the end of the day
you deserve
a man who stays.

We were two
hungry hearts
broken by past love
and brought together
for one reason
or another.

But my heart
was hungrier than yours
and in the end
you left me starving.

I adored him once
his sharp nose
his arrogant walk
but sometimes my heart
still fills with anger
with how
he treated me
and how
I let myself
be treated.

We were
a good-looking couple
on the outside
but in reality
that mess
was not
meant to be—
he couldn't
even tell me
he loved me.

I used to love
how you would
worship my body
and yet
you were the one
who told me
I put you up
on a pedestal.

I wanted to believe
we were a fairytale
where you saved me
from a lonely fate
because I thought
we were *magic*
except
there was no villain
just a lost prince
whose heart did not love
his wildfire princess.

PLANES

Watching you leave was like barely missing a flight. The adrenaline rush of sprinting to the gate, the quick moment of relief when I thought I would make it, then the brutal crash as I realized the plane was leaving without me.

You were the plane, and I was just another girl running through the airport.

For a brief moment, I thought we would make it.

I still smell
the essence of you
on my sheets
as I wrap myself
in them
falling asleep
to dreams
of you and me.

I lay in my bed
long after you left
knowing I'd never
see you again
and missing your body
so close to mine.

It's not fair
this timing
and as I cried
over the injustice
I slowly grew stronger
and emerged
from that day
with my heart focused
on the beautiful future
and learning to love
without you.

Becoming in Ballston

My heart
of fire and flame
has turned to ice
towards you
and there's no
going back.

You will never be
the partner I need
and losing you
was the best thing
to ever happen
to me.

It is time to leave
the past in the past
and write myself
an even better story.

I know he was toxic
but at the end of the day
a piece of me loved him
and that's hard to forget.

Today I am broken
but tomorrow
I will be gentle
I will be kind
and I will bloom again.

You burned through my heart
leaving scars I thought were love
but when the smoke cleared
there was only charred destruction.

He told me
that I was
too much
that I gave
too much
that I loved
too much.

But now I know
that *he* was
not enough.

I will never
apologize
for loving
too much.
Because
in the end
love is all
we have.

You thought
you were a
lighthouse
but even you
couldn't handle
my hurricane.

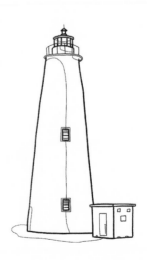

When it's over
you may cry yourself
to sleep at night
you may see his face
in every man you meet
you may cling
to old memories
just to hold onto
a piece of him
a little bit longer
but when it's all over
you'll be glad he's gone.

Becoming in Ballston

I let the memories of you
wash over me
but not drown me
as I slowly heal
from the love
I thought I knew.

Becoming in Ballston

I still remember
what it felt like
to love you
even though
that love
is now gone.

Sometimes I wonder
if you think about me
the way I think about you.
Or am I long forgotten
just another girl
from your past
nothing more
than another notch in your belt
just another girl
you've kissed
just another girl
you no longer miss.

I hope
when you look at
the ink on your arm
or when someone asks
you about it
or the next girl you love
runs her fingers across it
you'll think of me –
permanently.

Becoming in Ballston

I think
you will always seem
unreal to me —
my favorite summer fantasy.

For you seem
like a mythical beast
with only my memories
bringing you back.

I used to think
my heart
was made
of glass
the way it was
so easy
for you
to shatter it.

But in reality
my heart
is made
of fire and flame
and I burned
through the pain
you left
instead.

Becoming in Ballston

A piece of me died
when you left—
the fire within me
was extinguished.
But I've resurrected
from the ashes
a beautiful flaming beast
ready for new love—
one that I deserve.

– phoenix rising

I want to
adorn myself
in autumn leaves
let the wild wind
blow away
every memory
of you and me.

I thought I had
a second chance
at loving you
but really
it was just
another lesson
in letting you go.

Becoming in Ballston

I've burned
every memory of you
leaving behind
nothing but smoke
whose trail will soon fade
into the blue skies overhead.

The person
you are
means nothing
to me
anymore
but the feelings
you left
behind in your wake
still tear
me apart.

I can no longer feel
your touch
your hands
on my skin.

But sometimes
I still hear
your voice
on the wind.

But never worry,
I will forget.

Because I am far greater
than the love
you ever had to give.

– you are a mess of a man

Like the mountain
she rises above
every challenge
every mistake
every heartbreak.

We weren't meant
for each other
you weren't
my forever
I'm starting to realize
I'm okay with that.

I have shed
my past
I have grown
new skin
and I walk
into each day
full of gratitude
and excitement
for the beauty
and unknown
that is my future.

Revelations on Oxford Street

I used to be
addicted to leaving
I used to yearn
for people
who weren't meant
for me.

But now
I've learned
to live in the present
let it all go
and just breathe.

Sometimes I regret
letting you in again
but even though
I am angry
for the words you said
when you left
I cannot be mad
for the rest of it.

The scars
on my heart
are shaped
like your mouth.

You took more
than just a taste.

THE SCARS ON MY HEART

The scars on my heart are shaped like your mouth. You took more than just a taste. You left multiple bite wounds, some of which have only started to fade.

The largest one is from the day you left me speechless, the last time I saw you, the last time I will probably ever see you. You walked away and never looked back, left me there flailing, and I drove home with the same song on repeat, a song about a hurricane.

My favorite one is when I met you after dark on the stones of our college campus, when you were taking a break from studying in the library, and though I didn't know it then, I loved you. I loved you more than I had ever loved anyone before. And you kissed me on those forbidden stones while people ran by singing, "get a room," but you didn't care, we didn't care. All I cared about was you and the warmth between my legs, your lips on my neck.

The freshest one is from the summer before last. How you whisked me away to a magical fairytale land where time stood still, and it was just you and me and the woods. Time was our currency and I was greedy, surpassing my credit limit until suddenly, my week with you was over, and I found myself flying back to the other side of the country, without you.

After all that time
it was almost too easy
to drift into nothingness
and become strangers again.

How can someone
who once meant
the world to you
suddenly become
nothing but
a few memories?

The longing
for what
could have been
is what
breaks my heart
over again.

Hold my heart
please
take this burden
off of me.

– the heavy hearts club

AS THEY ARE

When our hearts are broken, it is often not the person we miss, but the relationship or the future we saw with them. We see people for their potential, not who they are in this present moment. And I think that is a big mistake. We have to start living in the here and now and accept people as they are.

I used to think
you saved me
but the truth of it is
I saved myself.

You were
just the spark
that started the fire—
the catalyst
to my new
beginning.

I wish I could tell you
how thankful I am for you
for helping me realize
what hell I was living in
as I saved myself.

I often thought
that forcing myself
to let go
was the answer

but what if instead of
pushing away those feelings
we just sit with them
and let them be.

For one summer
I believed
we could be
beautiful.

That was a lie
a sweet summer fantasy
for I realized
I could be beautiful
all on my own.

108

YOU CAME BACK FOR A REASON

I remember texting my best friend two words when I saw you again. It had been a few years since we had seen each other. "I'm screwed," I typed and hit send, then sat in my car for a long time, dreading the walk back into my apartment.

That day was the beginning of everything. I realized that I had been hiding the truth from myself and that my life needed to change.

Before, I never had the chance to get over you. And then, as if the Universe had planned it, you came back into my life. When I saw you again, I felt the old me, the girl I used to be and the girl I loved most, come back. You were new yet so familiar, and I could not get enough.

Before I saw you again, I had lost myself. After you, I wanted to find my way back. I felt hope again for the first time in a long while. The connection we had, the flirting, and the laughs we shared made me see what I was missing. I learned that *it is never too late to start over*.

In the end, you and I, we didn't work out. We broke up before for a reason, and those issues still applied years later. But I regret none of it.

You came back into my life to set me free. I used to think you saved me, but the truth of it is, I saved myself. You were just the catalyst to my new beginning.

Even though we did not work out, I needed you to come back into my life.

Single for the Summer in Clarendon

Heart pounding
nerves on fire
stomach churning
feelings rising
ones I haven't felt
in awhile
the constant questions
if he will like me
if I will like him
addicted to this thrill
as I begin again.

He cannot keep
his eyes off
the sway in my walk
the curve of my hips
as I dance away.

I know
he wants me
and he finds me
very tempting
but what
he doesn't know
is that he will never
catch me.

I know
I shouldn't do it
but it feels so good
naughty even
to be a wild child
throw caution to the wind
and get drunk
on your kiss.

I'm tired
of crying
over boys
because
I believed
they were men.

When did "let me walk you home" become code
word for sex?
When did a simple goodnight kiss become "let me
shove my tongue down her throat, in the hopes that
she'll invite me in"?
When did these become so common, that I've begun
to tire of my dating life?

When did chivalry die?

I'm so tired
of only being desired
for my body
and of falling
for boys
who aren't ready for me.

I'm so tired
of the games
and I'm ecstatic
to be free
and alone now
living just for me.

I've stopped looking
so hard for love
and instead
I'm letting love
find me.

I want a love that
shouts from the rooftops
holds me close in bed
wants to show me off
and will forever hold my hand.

For a long time
I wandered alone
avoiding the shifting sands
of midnight lovers' true intentions
searching only for
that blazing supernova love
to call my own.

Blue Ridge Blooming

She was in love
with the moon
the stars in the sky.

She was taken
by the earth
a wanderer wild.

The glow from
the southern sun
lit up her face
like a goddess divine.

I don't want
to be tamed
my fiery heart
cannot be contained.

I need to
be free to bloom
like a wildflower
among the weeds.

I am slowly learning
to relax
into my radiance
to forgive
the scars of the past
and to live
for the magic.

When the ocean's heart breaks
and the mermaid cries
her tears become sea glass—
a gentle reminder
that sometimes
beautiful things
come from pain.

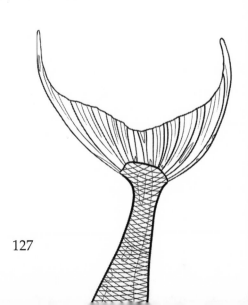

I am worth knowing
not for my long legs
not for my smile
but for the way
I try to see the light
in the never-ending dark
the way I strive
to build others up
the way I love
with everything I've got.

Letting go
of my need
for control
is the hardest
yet greatest thing
I've ever had to do.
It has cracked
my heart
wide-open.

It took me
a long time
but I finally met
people who
made me stop
craving you.

GOODBYE FOREVER

You have to come to terms with the truth: that them not loving you has *nothing to do with you*. It does not make you any less worthy of love, it does not mean you are not enough. It just means that they were not the right one for you. Know this: *it is okay that they did not love you*.

Only when
I accepted the end
of our story
was I able to begin
a new chapter
with a better man.

Home in Carolina

WHEN WE FIRST MET: THE LION

How I met you on a darkened street and how, as we walked together to a bar, I couldn't keep my eyes off you. How there was something so easy, so right, in your smile; I felt like I was coming home. How, by the end of the night, we were holding hands and laughing, and as you drove me back to my place, all I could think about was how badly I wanted to kiss you. How you walked me up to my door, and how you went for it, and how I haven't looked back since. How that night you became *my last first kiss*.

Everything
that I've been through
all made sense
when I met you.

Home in Carolina

My past
used to haunt me
but it led me to you
and my heart
has never been
this happy.

For those of us
who struggle
with love
I struggle
with being
overly critical
of overthinking
every. damn. thing.
of not
letting myself
be loved
the way
I need to be.

But with him
I feel seen
I feel heard
I feel respected
I feel loved.

When we try to make peace with our past, we have to go back into it. Sometimes, we have to relive it in order to let ourselves feel and heal from the memories we have pushed aside for too long. Fear often stops us here. Fear of being judged for the things we've done. Fear that our hearts won't stop hurting. But we have to do this work.

It's time to release the magic.

Darling
do not be afraid
to open your heart
or to walk away.

Whatever you choose
whenever you do
there is magic
waiting for you.

He likes to pull me in close
rub my nose against his
I didn't know love could be
sweet and tender like this.

– for my Leo

This is me
with all my past hurt
and all my demons
letting myself
open up
and fall for you.

Home in Carolina

I'm not sure
how he does it—
sees everything
about me
and still believes
that I'm beautiful.

143

You are sunshine
on a cold winter's day—
your warmth radiates
through my past and my pain.

Anchor me
to the depths
of the ocean
that is your wild heart.

I'm a boat
floating in the sea
tethered to your heart
I shall always be.

I knew
from the moment
we met
that my wild heart
had found
her home.

-November dreamers

I never thought
I'd love something as much
as the way
you hold my hand
and trace my palm
with your thumb
causing a cascade of sparks
to electrify my spine.

He sat there with me
as we watched
the rain fall
I breathed it in deeply
losing myself
to the beauty of it all
while he sat there quietly
he didn't judge me
he just let my wild
run free.

He loves my wild
instead of trying
to tame me.

148

I love you like
my heart is on fire
and I never want
this flame to die
I will always keep
a slow burn
an ember
in my heart
just for you.

You are
pure magic
the oxygen
to my fiery soul
I can't help
but be drawn to you.

I love you more
than I love
the stars in the sky
the song of the birds
welcoming the dawn
the magic of
a misty morning hike
through the woods
with not a sound
but those of nature
calling me home.
I love you more
than I love wandering.
And that's really
saying something.

YOU

You are baseball caps and worn college t-shirts. A morning cup of coffee—black, no sugar, no cream. Selfies with eyes closed and mouths open, laughing. Ice cream—no matter what the season. Tender kisses in the dark. Country songs on old dirt roads. A book I never want to close. Morning phone calls on the way to work. The sun on my face and the blue in the sky. My favorite hello and my hardest goodbye.

You are the greatest love.

Sometimes I feel
like I have lived
a thousand years
for all the people
who have touched
my soul.

Can I really hate
the path that got me here
when I'm so in love
with this destination?

THE END

Acknowledgements

I am incredibly thankful for the support I have received in publishing my first book. I have many to thank in my private life:

Dad, thank you for always pushing me to do my own thing.

Casey and Leo, the most important people in my life, thank you both for your love and always lifting me up.

Jules, thank you for your great friendship and all our fun adventures during our period of singleness together.

Kay, thank you for being my rock during our college years and beyond.

In terms of WANDERER's journey, I am grateful for my amazing editors who really brought the book together. I would also like to acknowledge the Instagram poetry community. Without their encouragement, I would not be here. I always say that it is the kindest, most uplifting group I have ever had the honor of interacting with. I am grateful for each and every one of you.

And of course, thank you, dearest reader, for going on this journey with me. WANDERER is for you.

About the Author

Court Young is a public health professional who has always loved reading and using her creative brain. An environmental health analyst by day, a writer by night, Court's writings have been featured in Thought Catalog, Unwritten, and on numerous poetry accounts.

Poetry is therapy for her, and she shares her writings with the world in the hopes that it will help others heal as well.

When not frantically writing in her Notes app, Court is often found outside, exploring and wandering, or visiting new local coffee shops in her home state of North Carolina.

WANDERER is Court's first book, which describes her journey of love and lust in her young adult life.

Instagram: @carolina_poetry

Website: www.courtyoung.com

Etsy Shop: Carolina Poetry Prints

Made in the USA
Las Vegas, NV
10 January 2022

41061229R00092